To Kate Klimo – JCA

To my best friend, Mark Radzinski – KR

Text copyright © 1989 by Jane Chelsea Aragon
Illustrations copyright © 1989 by Kandy Radzinski
All rights reserved.
Book design by Karen Pike
Printed in Hong Kong

Library of Congress Cataloging-in-Publication Data

Aragon, Jane Chelsea.
Lullaby/Jane Chelsea Aragon; illustrated by Kandy Radzinski.
p.   cm.
Summary: The notes of a lullaby, sung by a mother to her baby, are carried on the
wind and by small animals over towns, lakes, hills, through the night, until re-
turning on the breeze to the mother and child as a wake-up song.
ISBN 0-87701-576-7
[1. Lullabies.] I. Radzinski, Kandy, ill. II. Title.
PZ8.3.A57 Lu 1989
[E]—dc19   88-22685
                                                CIP
                                                AC

10   9   8   7   6   5   4   3   2   1

Chronicle Books
275 Fifth Street
San Francisco, California 94103

LULLABY

Jane Chelsea Aragon
Illustrations by Kandy Radzinski

To Alexander Matthew -
With love,
Jane
AUGUST 30, 1990

Chronicle Books • San Francisco

It started with the notes
of a lullaby,
the sweet, gentle rocking notes
of a mother singing her child to sleep.

The sleepy song was carried out on the wind,
over farmhouses and rooftops in villages and towns.

The windsong swept through meadows and woods,
drifting high above hills and mountains,
across lakes and rivers to the sea.

The sea heard the song
and sang it in sea-rhythms to the moon.
The moon echoed the melody in light rippling notes.
The whales in the sea heard the moonsong
and sang it deep under the water.

Boats at anchor heard the whales' song
and carried the tune on foghorns,
as they signaled to each other in the darkness.
The lighthouse keeper listened to the boats
and whistled the melody out into the foggy night.

A flock of wild geese traveling through the night sky
heard the lighthouse keeper's tune
and sang the song to the hills below.

In the hills a mockingbird heard the melody
and sang it to her babies in an evergreen tree.

The bullfrogs on the edge of the pond heard the mockingbird
and sang to the waterbirds who fell asleep on the shore.

The crickets in the woods listened to the bullfrogs' chorus
and chirped the lullaby to all the babies of the forest.
All through the meadows and all through the hills,
the lullaby was sung in the night.

And when the night ended and the sun began to rise,
the ducks on the pond quacked the melody
to one another in greeting.

Their wake-up song was heard by a little songbird,
who picked up the tune in its yellow beak
and flew away with it on the breeze—

to bring the morning song to a mother and a child,

waking to the new day.